Transformative Struggles of Hope, Unity and Solidarity

TSITSI GLADYS MADZONGWE

Copyright © 2025 Tsitsi Gladys Madzongwe.

All rights reserved. No part of this book may be reproduced, stored, or transmitted by any means—whether auditory, graphic, mechanical, or electronic—without written permission of both publisher and author, except in the case of brief excerpts used in critical articles and reviews. Unauthorized reproduction of any part of this work is illegal and is punishable by law.

ISBN: 979-8-89419-674-9 (sc)
ISBN: 979-8-89419-675-6 (hc)
ISBN: 979-8-89419-676-3 (e)

Because of the dynamic nature of the Internet, any web addresses or links contained in this book may have changed since publication and may no longer be valid. The views expressed in this work are solely those of the author and do not necessarily reflect the views of the publisher, and the publisher hereby disclaims any responsibility for them.

One Galleria Blvd., Suite 1900, Metairie, LA 70001
(504) 702-6708

PREFACE

Tsitsi Gladys Madzongwe is a Zimbabwean-American who migrated to the United States of America during the early seventies. Tsitsi have a firm belief that poetry is an art and movement whereby one can express their voice. She is compassionate about women, children, men, education, human poverty alleviation just to name a few. It is her firm belief that a wealth of human knowledge is lost when people stop expressing their voices. It is also her hope that individuals can feel emancipated from her spoken word. According to Tsitsi, profound social, economic and cultural change is attained through the spoken words that speak to our hearts and humanity. Pan Africanism is all about cultural regeneration and economic sustainability.

According to Tsitsi, writing this book has ensured her a place in paradise with clarity of vision to discern to what is going on in her life as a Pan Afrikan Poet.

REVIEWS

Tsitsi Madzongwe's Poetry is inspirational and rejuvineting. Her prose is more of a critic with an intention to disarm public awareness, economics, gender, social cultural awareness from a Global perspective.

Her Poetry reiterates stories of various cultures, women emancipation, love and humanity. Tsitsi Madzongwe interprets genuine democracy as everyone's responsibility.

—*Joyce Jenje Makwenda,*
Archivist Historian, Author & Ethno-Musicologist

Tsitsi's spoken words resonates with many folks in all walks of Life. The diversity of topics should inspire the world to understand the world that we live in and make this a better place.

—*Haki S. Ammi, Success Scholar*

Powerful, Timely and Provocative. Tsitsi Madzongwe moves us to open our minds and hearts in a quest to thoroughly examine the human condition

—*Phyllis Heller*

CONTENTS

HUMANITY 1
COLONIALISM 2
FREEDOM 4
PROFOUND WORDS 5
IDENTITY 7
GENDER IDENTITY 9
MIRROR ON THE WALL 10
ASSIMILATION 12
THE GHETTO 13
HOMELESSNESS 15
AMERICA 16
FAMINE 17
TRAFFICKING 18
SURVIVING THE STORM 19
I HAVE A DREAM 20
THE BLACK DRESS 21
THE AFRIKAN WOMAN 23
THE AFRIKAN MAN 24
HOPE 25
RAIN 27
THUNDERSTORMS 28
BLUE SKIES 29
THE SOLDIER 30
INTOLERANCE 31

NDATIIKO 32
ZIMBABWE 33
AFRICA 34
UNITY & FREEDOM 36
THE GLOBAL ECONOMY 37
AFRICAN SOVEREIGNTY 38
GLOBALIZATION 40
CHANGE 42
COURAGE 44
A WOMAN'S LOVE 45
EMANCIPATION 46
KINDNESS 47
AFRICAN PRIDE 49
THE NEW SONG 51
EMPATHY 52
RACE & ETHNICITY 53
HAPPINESS 55

HUMANITY

Ancient Africa tells us a story about the beginning of Humanity.
Human legacy is Africa's ancient story.
Africa's history's early stories resonate traditions,
religion, culture and art.

Culture is humanity.
It manifests collectivity,
and in turn,
Collectivity creates productivity and development against every system of oppression.

Humanity pushes back historical dictatorship.
There is a priority need for economic self-sufficiency and sustainability.
Environmental degradation will not be tolerated.
Humanity demands respect and dignity.
Generational voices strike the urgency of time
in rebellion and victory!

COLONIALISM

Most Global institutions are structured to keep Africa
Impoverished with its raw materials.
Colonialism is a perfect blend that harmonizes
with imperialism.
Colonialism is a symbol of European global power.

The Slave trade altered the Continent's culture and history.
European powers exploited the African indigenous.
They pushed their economic resources and portioned the
African economic development system.

Unbalanced trade systems suppressed the integration
of the Continent.
Colonialism perpetuated foreign markets from the Continent's
cheap labor and raw materials goods.
Colonialism subjected the Continent into a Global world economic
system.

Colonialism caused famine and hunger.
It brought Foreign Taxation to the Continent and its citizens.
Africans were not equal to foreign trade.
They couldn't move their commodities.
They had no substantial community wealth infrastructures.

Colonialism connects humanity with brave unstoppable passion.
The rich declare war on the poor.
Colonialism sparks flames of purpose and a sense of idealism.

"Enough is Enough.. Africa contributed to Europe's economic recovery. So why does it remain poor?..We are the original people and we have every reason to stand up on the tallest mountains to proclaim who we are...We are beautiful, intelligent, sophisticated, highly adaptable and totalling indestructible people-the Africans."

Dr. Arikana Chihombori-Quao

FREEDOM

Colonization and Imperialism is terror.
Colonization and Imperialism is horrific.
Cries and emotions of devastation
are heard everywhere.
Earthly pain is felt everywhere.

The thoughts are soaring,
And the heart is broken.
Alone and detached, the indigenous has lost hope.
Tear drops are falling, and devastation is felt everywhere.

Emancipation has become an unachievable goal.
A voice whispers,
"Arise and be an example unto me.
Follow my footsteps.
Sorrow is not to be appeased."

Strength is in your honor.
Time is of the essence.
Freedom is not to be compromised.

PROFOUND WORDS

Profound words enchant the soul and spirit.
Profound words are vibrant and stir the images
of the mind.
Profound words embrace individuals with compassion.
They emancipate individuals from bondage, storms
and circumstances.

Profound words whisper melodies of love.
They enchant rainbow colors and heal every wound.
Profound words enable reality to shift your life
with favor and bliss.

Profound words are powerful.
They shape a person's destiny.
They instill and create an individual's path with sovereignty.
Profound words manifest abundance and prosperity!

"Stand up straight and realize who you are, that you tower over your circumstances."

Maya Angelo

IDENTITY

Identity has a special meaning.
Identity has a special meaning
to a man, woman, child, and every human being.
Identity reinforces the human bonds
between self and ancestry.

Identity, power and culture are
synonymous characteristics
that explore and integrate
an individual's identity.

Identity is impressive.
It conveys hope, dignity
and independence.

Identity is a symbol
of modern society a
and culture.

"Power is the ability not just to tell the story of another person, but to make it the definitive story of that person"

Chimamanda Ngozi Adichie

GENDER IDENTITY

Gender Identity is synonymous to economic superiority.
Culture and tradition has led to the inheritance of gender identity
Gender Identity can consume feelings of either
joy, anxiety, depression or fulfillment.
Gender Identity is a roaring fire of courage In an individual's space.

Gender Identity is an abstract landscape of how one can go above
and beyond their expectations.
Liberty and equality ignites a person's dreams and hope.
Gender Identity enables one to share the Global world with everyone
in it's existence.

MIRROR ON THE WALL

Mirror, mirror on the wall,
Who am I when I look
at the mirror on the wall?
Is my race a campaign
of oppression or genocide?
Is the color of my skin
The struggle of my existence, or due
to the warm temperatures of my
African inheritance?

Mirror, mirror on the wall
Is race and identity synonymous?
Is race a meaningful concept,
Or a useful heuristic method?

Mirror, mirror on the wall,
Is my race social or scientific?
Is it blood in my veins,
and what ought I to be?
I ask again, is it by choice,
Or by the creation of the Master?

Mirror, mirror on the wall,
Does my skin color convey
wisdom or favor?
Is it barbaric or civilized?
Mirror, mirror on the wall,
race and identity
are the Master's skill.
and a heuristic method.
Race and identity
are the Master's skill, and not the configurations
of my friends and society.

"Never share your dreams and hopes with people who doubt your potential and have no ability to think beyond limitations. Those who have made it Big were told that it's impossible."

Maponga Joshua

ASSIMILATION

Colonialism, slavery and historical anachronisms visualizes
horror for the immigrant.
Assimilation enables the immigrant to be part of
a homogenous culture.
Assimilation and diversity is the impediment of hope
in the midst of adversity.

Cultural integration is all about our ancestors.
Cultural integration is a way of life.
It's about the way people eat, talk, dress and worship.

The immigrant should learn how to embrace humanity
and public service.
The immigrant can be content in their own culture,
social and economic realms.
Who is to say there's a right or way of doing things.
The immigrant rises because of their own identity and culture.
Cultural integration is all about a way of life!

THE GHETTO

Each day is like a nightmare.
There are no family traditions
to hold onto.

The family is split apart.
The roots of the African and European
ancestors have been shattered.

Unemployment is skyrocketing.
The streets are full of drugs
and loose trash.

Men and women are homeless.
Misery, depression, sickness
and poverty have become epidemics
in the Ghetto.

The poor remain insignificant.
They feel no reason to exist.
Most individuals have become
anxious and hopeless.
Time is not moving fast enough
for change to occur.

Only the redeemed can survive.
America the land of opportunity
has become an illusion.

"For there's always light, if only we're brave enough to see it. If only we're brave enough to be it."

Amanda Gorman

"I'm not going to be a victim; I'm going to be part of the solution, and when I rise, I rise and I rise with others."

Dr. Tererai Trent

HOMELESSNESS

Homelessness causes you to shout for help.
The concrete beneath a homeless person's barefeet
or wornout shoes is unbearable.
Homelessness makes individuals feel angry as the cars passby and
noone is paying attention or acknowledging their dilemma.
Homelessness causes individuals to shout for help.
Homelessness oppresses individuals.
Knowing that someone cares enables the homeless to have hope.
With resilience and hope, the homeless can face tomorrow
and the days ahead of their lives.

AMERICA

O, America, the land of the immigrant...
O, America, the land of liberty...
O, America, home of prosperity...
O, America, the world's superpower...
O, America, what has happened to you?

O, America, unemployment
Is at its highest level.
O, America there is uncertainty
for surviving the future.
O, America Wall Street is crushing
and is out of control.
O, America, what has happened
to our industrial base?

O, America, fear and anxiety
are overwhelming our leaders.
O, America, there is hostility
among the people.
O, America, what will sustain the future generation?

O, America, land and home of the free,
There is great hope
that economic restoration
is on the way.

FAMINE

Poverty remains a leading cause
of death in Africa.
The land is full of thorns, diseases and famine.

The people are bitter and angry at each other.
The vultures are feasting
and the children are crying.
Their dreams are shattered because they
may never see tomorrow.

Looters don't care about anyone or their own.
Transparency and equality are Africa's
only hope for tomorrow

TRAFFICKING

At Sunset the deal is striked.
Pretty ladies are roaming the streets.
They are flirting with lovely men.

At Sunset the price is right.
At Sunset she awaits impatiently for
that stroke that preserves his sanity.

Scooping up on a moonlight bath and dinner
subdued by the naked body,
She is anticipating how she is going to pay her bills,
She is anticipating how she is going to feed
and pay her children's school fees.

The chains have shifted from soft body to
mimicking his insecurities.
The woman has been pampered by others
but mocked by what has been written on her skin.

The night is ugly, merciless with continuous and
countless tricks.
The question to ask is ….
At sunset are women alone in action and or by choice ?
Do they need to stand together to prevail their essential roles
as mothers or caretakers of their children?
Most women stand together in expression joined by
an empathetic voice to sustain life beyond their boundaries.

SURVIVING THE STORM

Storms blow their way own energy.
Winds blow their own aroma.
The road is covered with thorns
and humility.
People are crying for deliverance
from their enemies.
Storms are continuous.
Resilience and perseverance are
the only way to fulfill an individual's
dream.
Resilience and perseverance
is the only way to find purpose and hope
for tomorrow.

I HAVE A DREAM

I have a dream....
I have a dream of the sweat of my
forefathers,
A dream to reclaim
that which is my own.

I have a dream....
I have a dream authenticated
by my Creator.
A dream to mount up like an eagle
in every circumstance.

I have a dream...
that God will fulfill
the desires of my heart.
I have a dream to uphold
that which is precious to me.

THE BLACK DRESS

The woman dressed in a black dress
is a companion to everyone.
Ablaze in fire and cool as a cucumber,
she is like a torch
that sails above the earth.

Her name whispers a lullaby
to those who know her.
Her hair is kinky and curly.
Her emotions are delicate.

She shakes her head and says,
"No" to pain and suffering,
"No" to exploitation,
"No" to racism,
"No" to poverty,
"No" to sexism,
Hope and prosperity
are within her reach.

The woman dressed in a black dress
is tall and curvy.
Her skin is radiant,
It is like silk to touch.
It casts everything
In bronze.
Her perfume
invigorates the senses.

The woman dressed in a black dress
has an ancient voice that cradles the ears.
Her voice is full of wisdom.
Her wisdom shines and soothes generations
to come.

Solidarity is her nature.
Her brown eyes are far-fetching.
At dusk, they convey love for mankind.

THE AFRIKAN WOMAN

She is like a brick house.
Strength and honor are her compassion.
Her body is like a pillar of strength.
At the crack of dawn,
she is her children's only hope
for food and shelter.
She is humble and humiliated.
Her dreams are of hope and unification.

As blood runs through her veins,
she is resilient
and illuminated with strength.
She stumbles and falls,
but she rises again.
She stands upright during a turbulent force.
Her smile is illuminated with strength and honor.
Her wisdom is focused.
Afrikan woman is bold and resilient.

Afrikan woman is like a fallen hero.
Her wisdom is her strength.
It ascends from her spiritual being.

THE AFRIKAN MAN

His eyes are piercing.
His smile is illuminating.
His voice is wisdom.
His children call him blessed.

The Afrikan man is not contentious.
He is not divisive,
rather he avoids disputes.

The Afrikan man does not cry,
wail or groan.
His sword and blade are always ready.
These are symbols of protection and love
for his family and community.

The Afrikan man's integrity
survives the test of time.
His stature is an armor of strength.
His demeanor is love for all mankind.

HOPE

There is hope for tomorrow.
There is hope for
the men, women
and children, who are dying
of hunger and poverty.

The rivers are overflowing.
The birds are singing.
They are humming the quaintest lullabies.

The trees are shaking and standing.
The birds are building nests
full of treasures.
The only hope is to try again
to plant and reap a harvest.

"Education is the quite seed that grows into a forest of possibilities, lighting paths where none seemed to exist, and turning every learner into both a dreamer and a builder of tomorrow."

Dr. Christina Cutlip

RAIN

Rain overcomes the stilled winds.
Rain quenches the spirit.
Rain redeems the pulses of hunger.
It washes out drought and prepares
for the harvest.

Rain shortens the time of hunger.
It makes you burst from within.
Rain is abundant life.
It ruptures thirst and hunger.

Rain binds despair and sadness.
It settles the circling spirit within us!

THUNDERSTORMS

Love is illuminated
in the striking lightning.
Triumph is felt
in the welcome sound of thunder.

Reassurance and confirmation
defeat despair.
Reassurance promises harvests
and prosperity.

Precipitation yields grain.
The seeds are sprouting.
There is a feeling of tenderness.

The breath of air is exalted.
Thunderstorms unleash
the inhabitant's inner strengths.
Thunderstorms are swift to soothe.

BLUE SKIES

Today the sky is blue,
the gardens are stuttering
with roses and African violets.

The birds are chirping:
"How do you do?"
They are flying like
signal flares asking,
"Are you happy, sad, lucky,
poor, rich or famous?"

Tell the birds your flavor
as they spread their wings
and fly around.
Is it the past, or the future,
as you look up to the skies?

The immense blue sky
wipes away every sorrow
with a white chalkboard of clouds.

THE SOLDIER

The death of an upright man with dignity
has inflicted pain.
Pain to his country and beloved family.

How can Africa turn away
From a man of such great compassion.
Who would exchange
compassion for grief?

Evil has betrayed the wife, the husband, the son,
the daughter, the father, the mother, the aunt,
the uncle and above all,
The soldier who lies in darkness.

The fields are empty.
A smell of burning fire arouses the nose.
The fields are scattered with ashes.
The evergreen crops echo a farewell
to a great soldier.

Outside they are yelling,
"Come here, you boy,
Where were you when he needed you?"

The country is dancing to ritualistic music.
The sounds of the drums evoke the spirit.
The beer is brewing,
men and women are drunk and reminiscing.

Memories linger as Africa finds its strength
from a great soldier.
The song never ends.
Heaven-bound, melodies of gratitude are heard in Zion.

INTOLERANCE

Intolerance is violent and potent.
Intolerance is suspicious and vicious.
It is idealized and ignorant.

Intolerance is barbaric.
Intolerance is a powerful source
of mob mentality.

Intolerance must be taught against
locally, and in each family, school,
village and country.

It's formation
cannot be tolerated.

NDATIIKO

Do you know what Ndatiiko means?
Ndatiiko is a She Hero who has globally inspired many
other individuals.
Ndatiiko means to listen and remain steadfast during
a turbulent storm.
A painful separation from discrimination, colonialization and racism
is a bursting initiative of womanhood.
Ndatiiko can withstand a painful season with hope and resilience.

Ndatiiko represents a woman in all spheres of life.
Ndatiiko is a painful separation from gender equality
and racism.
She is a bursting initiative of womanhood.
Ndatiiko erects equality for her children and future generations.
Ndatiiko celebrates Unity and represents her Nation
and the various global communities.

Ndatiiko is a slab of granite that is etched in culture and honor.
Ndatiiko can get to any place she wants in life without any
hesitation.
She brings joy, laughter and wisdom to everyone's womanhood.
Humanity and genuine democracy ignite her purpose in life.

ZIMBABWE

Zimbabwe is a house of stones that has bold species of ancestral culture and christianity.
The Kingdom of Zimbabwe has unmatched stones in the entire world.
Zimbabwe stones are comparable to today's purpose.

Zimbabwe is my ancestral house built upon a rock.
Zimbabwe is an epidement of civilization, culture and economic prosperity.
It is a host land of gold, lithium, agricultural farming and diamonds.
Economic sanctions were implemented to exploit the poor people.

Zimbabwe is a resilient house of stones.
Exploitation has restructured Zimbabwe's prosperity.
Mandatory transparent and economic restoration is the only hope for Zimbabwe.

AFRICA

Africa my motherland
Africa is a country that echoes ancient wisdom.
Africa is a country that embraces our hearts
with rainbow colors.

Africa my motherland, your resources are
a treasure that cannot be compromised.
Africa you are a gift to the Human Race.
At Sunrise the sun announces it's presence
and promises.
At Sunset the skies are soothing and provide
safety for the human race.
Africa, you enchant and provoke trade
and economic prosperity.

"Economic empowerment is the foundation of true freedom. When people control their resources, they control their future."

Dr. Stella Jeffries

UNITY & FREEDOM

Unity and freedom is to reflect and act in the moment.
Unity and freedom is strength and empowerment.
Unity and freedom is the beginning of an era.

Unity and freedom is to dance and shout freedom and victory.
Unity and freedom is a fresh voice.
It is a new hope of what gives individuals strength.

Unity and freedom sings a song of sacrifice.
It tells the tales of an individual's blood and sweat.

Unity and freedom enables an individual to tell the tales
of eclipse and the tales of the seed that has been crushed
to earth.
With unity and freedom, we can rise together as a people
and a Nation.

THE GLOBAL ECONOMY

The economy's formula out of balance.
Fathers, mother, and children are tormented.
The world is grieving with a wish and hope.

The rich are threatening the poor.
There is a fall in demand.
Prosperity for the working poor
has become the thing of the past.
The hour and the moment conveys pain
and suffering for the world.

The rich are unconcerned.
They continue to build
and preserve their nests.
Finding a solution has become an adventure
for the experts and policy makers.

AFRICAN SOVEREIGNTY

Urbanization is escalating as people migrate from rural areas
in pursuit of jobs.
Elitism and ignorance on governing the Continent has
become a major task.
Hunger, unemployment and medical care are major necessities
around the Continent.
Political and economic freedom are not aligned.

The African Sovereignty is the willingness to discern and
staying focused on the humanitarian solutions of its people.
Democracy and economic prosperity is attained when people
Have affection and tolerance for one another.

Resilience is the ability to overcome every adversity and challenge.
Freedom, peace and equality is what Africa needs.

"Zimbabwe has fought & won more wars than any other country in Africa. We have a Tribalism problem enabling colonial divisions. Courage is to embrace Humanity"

Rutendo Matinyarare

GLOBALIZATION

Globalization is all about new markets competition.
Globalization allows countries to create and explore various technologies and industries.

Globalization allows free trade.
It creates wealth for the poor.
It upgrades their standard of living through economic transformation and diversification of resources.
Innovation is a spirit of adventure!

"If you want a break with Imperialist forces, you must denounce the Colonial Defence Agreements...Those Imperialists consider that we belong to them , and that our wealth belongs to them. They think they can continue to tell us what is good for our States. Africa, our Continent suffered so much because of the Imperialists. This era is gone forever, our resources will remain for us and our populations."

President Ibrahim Traore

CHANGE

Change inspires individuals and communities.
Change is synonymous with creating a harmonious culture for individuals and their communities.

Change is about you as an individual.
Change is when you look back and see where you have been.
Change is when you look forward with uncertainty.
Artificial Intelligence in various Global sectors are all trends of change and the future.

Looking at life's experiences and encounters as unnecessary struggles prevents us to be receptive to its marvels.

Change allows an individual to never be frightened with what lies ahead.
Change is the ability to withstand every obstacle and staying focused on your dreams and goals.

"Change will not come if we wait for some other person, or if we wait for some other time. We are the ones we've been waiting for. We are the Change that we seek."

President Barack Obama

COURAGE

Courage is an act of humanity.
Courage is living
in the moment
and achieving a purpose.

To be courageous is
to do something for others
and not worry about
what others can do for you.
Courage is living a daily race
against the clock.

To be courageous is to embrace
humanity and achieve a
ripe overflowing harvest.

A WOMAN'S LOVE

A woman's love is endless to her children, husband,
family and community.
A woman is a treasure from God.
She is the fruit tree of fortune and
a lusture of the full moon.
A woman's love gives strength to all Nations.
A woman's love is something no one can dismiss.

Life is barrier without a woman's love.
A woman's love can never be exposed with a
human eye.
A woman's love can never be exposed with a
human eye.
A woman's love is uplifting and soothing.
A woman's love is endless and widespread.

A woman's love is sublime.
It is universal and pure.
It shields everyone regardless of any circumstances.
A woman's love is a song full of joy.
A woman's love is a stream of virtual beauty.

EMANGIPATION

The Black people are the Ancestors of Humanity.
The Ancestors of Humanity were discovered in Africa.
The Ancestors of Humanity were the first inventors.
Africans were the greatest Scholars.

Africans could write before the Missionary ships arrived.
Abraham Lincoln freed the blacks in America.
Emancipation cannot be compromised.
Ancestors are the only ones who can intercede with
the Creator in our favor.

The black skin color is not a curse.
The establishment of poverty is not
subjective but objective.
The Black communities need to educate
and collaborate with each other.
Unity and empowerment can guarantee
survival and favor for the black communities.

KINDNESS

Acts of kindness
cause old resentments
to be absolved.

Acts of kindness
make justice soften
a hard heart.

Acts of kindness
cause peace to transform
darkness into light.

Acts of kindness
give hope, inspiration
and empowerment.

Acts of kindness
Makes a community breathe
one breath.

Acts of kindness
makes every person see
the world's beauty.

"The key to success is Unity. We need to build collaborations. The hood has been comfortable for most black people. We have embraced so much pain but now we have to live on legacy. The impact you put on earth stays forever."

Akon Thiam

AFRICAN PRIDE

African Pride is the vision of the Continent renewed.
African Pride is the right of the freedom of expression.
A new vision is anticipated.
A new Africa is born.
African pride conveys communication between its leaders
and its citizens.
African Pride does not cause conflict.
It enhances partnerships and shares the common ideals of humanity.

African Pride is all about diversity and National pride.
It is all about tolerance and mutual respect.
African Pride is a connection and continuity about
who we are as people.
It overcomes gender differences and prejudice.
African Pride is autonomic and redefines a sense of
universality.
African Pride is a tale that is told with a harvest!

"My generation does not understand this: how can Africa which has so much wealth, become the poorest Continent in the world today?"

President Ibrahim Traore

THE NEW SONG

The new song ravishes my heart as I awake at
at the cracker dawn.
Alone in the gloom my soul is bare.

The rhythms of the new song make my cheeks blush.
The rhythms of the new song devour my heart with
feelings of gladness.
It's a song that ignites and subdues my inner being.
It's rhythms and lyrics gives me strength.
The new song absorbs my heart and fears.

The new song quietly makes me reflect back to my
childhood years as I imagine my grandmother cradling
me in her arms by the fireside.

In reverence of the past, I find contentment in my inner
being for I know that I am not alone.
When dusk starts to unfold, the new song fills my heart
with sunshine.

EMPATHY

The Blacks were regarded as a commodity by the
Colonialists and Slave Masters.
Empathy is powerful when one emerges
from racism and other emotional torture reminders.
Empathy allows people to reflect on their
daily failures and experiences.

Empathy challenges people to see things
from a different perspective.
It teaches individuals to be courageous
and to set boundaries.

Empathy is essential for our communities
and the Global world.
Empathy fosters teamwork and generosity.
Empathy reinforces collaboration and unity.

RACE & ETHNICITY

Is race and ethnicity color blind?
Immigration comprises newborn native populations
in every country around the world.
Throughout history across the board, Colonialism
and Anglo-Saxonism has played a role on defining
individuals.

From the Colonization and Slavery days, black
people have been told that they are inferior
to their slave masters.
Race and Ethnicity is expressed in the absurd
theory of the poverty establishment and the dependence
of the welfare system.

Borders cannot chain an individual's passions and dreams.
Race is equal from a biological and Christianity perspective.
Racial identity supports and validates political and economic
power on individuals and their governments. Political, economic
and cultural solidarity enables society to achieve humanity
and deter racism.

Integration of every race brings opportunity for the immigrant.
Assimilation and diversity infuses inter-racial cultural power
and racial solidarity.

"It's freedom for everybody or freedom for nobody. We have a common oppressor, a common explorer, and a common discriminator. But once we all realize that we have this common enemy, then we unite on the basis of what we have in common."

Malcom X

HAPPINESS

Happiness is peace that surpasses
every understanding.
Happiness is joy unspeakable full of glory.
Happiness is tolerance, perseverance,
brotherhood, sisterhood,
and generosity.

Happiness is never to give up.
Happiness is the right to food and water.
Happiness is the right to education.
Happiness is the right to free and fair trade.
Happiness is the right to equality and
freedom of expression.

Happiness is the balance
between truth and justice.
Happiness is self-control and dignity.
Happiness is spontaneity!

www.ingramcontent.com/pod-product-compliance
Lightning Source LLC
LaVergne TN
LVHW091536070526
838199LV00001B/91